JESUS PARABLES

JESUS
PARABLES

Aivan Sunday

INTRODUCTION

When we have an understanding of the parables of Jesus, we receive knowledge and a clear insight into the mystery of God's kingdom to come to a perfect understanding of life. The parables of Jesus embody much of his fundamental teachings. They are the words of God the Father. Then said Jesus unto them, "When ye have lifted up the Son of man, then shall ye know that I am he and that I do nothing of myself, but as my Father hath taught me, I speak these things" (John 8:28).

Jesus parables contain great volumes of truth in very few words, and His parables, rich in imagery, are not easily forgotten. So then, the parable is a blessing to those with willing ears. But to those with dull hearts and ears that are slow to hear, the parable is also an instrument of judgment and mercy. To those with a genuine hunger for God, the parable is an effective and memorable vehicle for the conveyance of divine truths.

Jesus was the master of teaching through parables. His sayings were cleverly designed to draw listeners into new ways of thinking, new attitudes, and new ways of acting.

THE WISE AND FOOLISH BUILDERS

Matthew 7:24–27

—❧—

KJV—24 Therefore, whosoever heareth these sayings of mine and doeth them, I will liken him unto a wise man, which built his house upon a rock. 25 And the rain descended, and the floods came, and the winds blew and beat upon that house, and it fell not, for it was founded upon a rock. 26 And every one that heareth these sayings of mine and doeth them not shall be likened unto a foolish man, which built his house upon the sand. 27 And the rain descended, and the floods came, and the winds blew and beat upon that house, and it fell, and great was the fall of it.

Amp—24 So everyone who hears these words of mine and acts upon them, obeying them, will be like a sensible, prudent, practical, wise man who built his house upon the rock. 25 And the rain fell, and the floods came, and the winds blew and beat against that house, yet it did not fall, because it had been founded on the rock. 26 And everyone who hears these words of mine and does not do them will be like a stupid, foolish man who built his house upon the sand. 27 And the rain fell, and the floods came, and the winds blew and beat against that house, and it fell, and great and complete was the fall of it.

THE CHILDREN IN THE MARKETPLACE

Matthew 11:16–19

KJV—16 But whereunto shall I liken this generation? It is like unto children sitting in the markets and calling unto their fellows 17 and saying, "We have piped unto you, and ye have not danced; we have mourned unto you, and ye have not lamented." 18 For John came neither eating nor drinking, and they say, "He hath a devil." 19 The Son of man came eating and drinking, and they say, "Behold, a man gluttonous, and a winebibber, a friend of publicans and sinners." But wisdom is justified of her children.

Amp—16 But to what shall I liken this generation? It is like little children sitting in the marketplaces who call to their playmates: 17 "We piped to you, playing wedding, and you did not dance; we wailed dirges, playing funeral, and you did not mourn and beat your breasts and weep aloud." 18 For John came neither eating nor drinking with others, and they say, "He has a demon!" 19 The Son of man came eating and drinking with others, and they say, "Behold, a glutton and a wine drinker, a friend of tax collectors and especially wicked sinners!" Yet wisdom is justified and vindicated by what she does her deeds and by her children.

THE STRONGMAN BOUND

Matthew 12:29

—⚭—

KJV—29 Or else, how can one enter into a strongman's house and spoil his goods, except he first bind the strongman? And then he will spoil his house.

Amp—29 Or how can a person go into a strongman's house and carry off his goods—the entire equipment of his house—without first binding the strongman? Then, indeed, he may plunder his house.

The Unclean Spirit

Matthew 12:43–45

KJV—43 When the unclean spirit is gone out of a man, he walketh through dry places, seeking rest and findeth none. 44 Then he saith, "I will return into my house from whence I came out," and when he is come, he findeth it empty, swept, and garnished. 45 Then goeth he and taketh with himself seven other spirits more wicked than himself, and they enter in and dwell there: and the last state of that man is worse than the first. Even so shall it be also unto this wicked generation.

Amp—43 But when the unclean spirit has gone out of a man, it roams through dry arid places in search of rest, but it does not find any. 44 Then it says, "I will go back to my house from which I came out." And when it arrives, it finds the place unoccupied, swept, put in order, and decorated. 45 Then it goes and brings with it seven other spirits more wicked than itself, and they go in and make their home there. And the last condition of that man becomes worse than the first. So also shall it be with this wicked generation.

THE SOWER

Matthew 13:3–23

KJV—3 And he spake many things unto them in parables, saying, "Behold, a sower went forth to sow, 4 and when he sowed, some seeds fell by the way side, and the fowls came and devoured them up. 5 Some fell upon stony places, where they had not much earth, and forthwith they sprung up, because they had no deepness of earth. 6 And when the sun was up, they were scorched, and because they had no root, they withered away. 7 And some fell among thorns, and the thorns sprung up, and choked them. 8 But others fell into good ground and brought forth fruit, some an hundredfold, some sixtyfold, some thirtyfold. 9 Who hath ears to hear, let him hear." 10 And the disciples came and said unto him, "Why speakest thou unto them in parables?" 11 He answered and said unto them, "Because it is given unto you to know the mysteries of the kingdom of heaven, but to them it is not given. 12 For whosoever hath, to him shall be given, and he shall have more abundance, but whosoever hath not, from him shall be taken away even that he hath. 13 Therefore speak I to them in parables, because they seeing see not, and hearing they hear not, neither do they understand. 14 And in them is fulfilled the prophecy of Esaias, which saith, 'By hearing ye shall hear and shall not understand, and seeing ye shall see and shall not perceive.' 15 For this, people's heart is waxed gross, and their ears are dull of hearing, and their eyes they have closed; lest at any time they should see with their eyes and hear with their ears and should understand with their heart and should be converted and I should heal them. 16 But blessed are your eyes, for they see, and your ears, for they hear. 17 For verily I say unto you that many prophets and righteous men have desired to see those things which ye see and have not seen them and to hear those things which ye hear and have not heard them. 18 Hear ye therefore the parable of the sower. 19 When anyone heareth the word of the kingdom and understandeth it not, then cometh the wicked one and catcheth away that which was sown in his heart. This is he which received seed by the way side. 20 But he that received the seed into stony places, the same is he that heareth the word and anon with joy receiveth it. 21 Yet hath he not root in himself but dureth for a while, for when tribulation or persecution ariseth because of the word, by and by he is offended. 22 He also that received seed among the thorns is he that heareth the word and the care of this world, and the deceitfulness of riches choke the word, and he becometh unfruitful. 23 But he that received seed into the good ground is he that heareth the word and understandeth it, which also beareth fruit and bringeth forth, some an hundredfold, some sixty, some thirty."

Amp—3 And He told them many things in parables stories by way of illustration and comparison, saying, "A sower went out to sow. 4 And as he sowed, some seeds fell by the roadside, and the birds came and ate them up. 5 Other seeds fell on rocky ground, where they had not much soil, and at once they sprang up because they had no depth of soil. 6 But when the sun rose, they were scorched, and because they had no root, they dried up and withered away. 7 Other seeds fell among thorns, and the thorns grew up and choked them out. 8 Other seeds fell on good soil and yielded grain—some a hundred times as much as was sown, some sixty times as much, and some thirty. 9 He who has ears to hear, let him be listening, and let him consider and perceive and comprehend by hearing." 10 Then the disciples came to him and said, "Why do you speak to them in parables?" 11 And he replied to them, "To you it has been given to know the secrets and mysteries of the kingdom of heaven, but to them it has not been given. 12 For whoever has spiritual knowledge, to him will more be given, and he will be furnished richly so that he will have abundance, but from him who has not, even what he has will be taken away. 13 This is the reason that I speak to them in parables: because having the power of seeing, they do not see, and having the power of hearing, they do not hear, nor do they grasp and understand. 14 In them, indeed, is the process of fulfillment of the prophecy of Isaiah, which says: 'You shall, indeed, hear and hear but never grasp and understand, and you shall, indeed, look and look but never see and perceive.' 15 For this nation's heart has grown gross, fat, and dull, and their ears heavy and difficult of hearing, and their eyes they have tightly closed, lest they see and perceive with their eyes and hear and comprehend the sense with their ears and grasp and understand with their heart and turn, and I should heal them. 16 But blessed happy, fortunate, and to be envied are your eyes because they do see and your ears because they do hear. 17 Truly I tell you, many prophets and righteous men—men who were upright and in right standing with God—yearned to see what you see and did not see it and to hear what you hear and did not hear it. 18

Listen then to the meaning of the parable of the sower: 19 While anyone is hearing the word of the kingdom and does not grasp and comprehend it, the evil one comes and snatches away what was sown in his heart. This is what was sown along the roadside. 20 As for what was sown on thin rocky soil, this is he who hears the word and at once welcomes and accepts it with joy, 21 Yet it has no real root in him but is temporary, inconstant, lasts but a little while, and when affliction or trouble or persecution comes on account of the word, at once he is caused to stumble; he is repelled and begins to distrust and desert him whom he ought to trust and obey, and he falls away. 22 As for what was sown among thorns, this is he who hears the word, but the cares of the world and the pleasure and delight and glamour and deceitfulness of riches choke and suffocate the word, and it yields no fruit. 23 As for what was sown on good soil, this is he who hears the word and grasps and comprehends it; he, indeed, bears fruit and yields in one case a hundred times as much as was sown, in another sixty times as much, and in another thirty."

THE WEEDS

Matthew 13:24–30

KJV—24 Another parable put he forth unto them, saying, "The kingdom of heaven is likened unto a man which sowed good seed in his field. 25 But while men slept, his enemy came and sowed tares among the wheat and went his way. 26 But when the blade was sprung up and brought forth fruit, then appeared the tares also. 27 So the servants of the householder came and said unto him, 'Sir, didst not thou sow good seed in thy field? from whence then hath it tares?' 28 He said unto them, 'An enemy hath done this.' The servants said unto him, 'Wilt thou then that we go and gather them up?' 29 But he said, 'Nay, lest while ye gather up the tares, ye root up also the wheat with them. 30 Let both grow together until the harvest, and in the time of harvest, I will say to the reapers, "Gather ye together first the tares, and bind them in bundles to burn them, but gather the wheat into my barn."'"

Amp—24 Another parable He set forth before them, saying, "The kingdom of heaven is like a man who sowed good seed in his field. 25 But while he was sleeping, his enemy came and sowed also darnel weeds resembling wheat among the wheat and went on his way. 26 So when the plants sprouted and formed grain, the darnel weeds appeared also. 27 And the servants of the owner came to him and said, 'Sir, did you not sow good seed in your field? Then how does it have darnel shoots in it?' 28 He replied to them, 'An enemy has done this.' The servants said to him, 'Then do you want us to go and weed them out?' 29 But he said, 'No, lest in gathering the wild wheat weeds resembling wheat, you root up the true wheat along with it. 30 Let them grow together until the harvest, and at harvest time, I will say to the reapers, "Gather the darnel first and bind it in bundles to be burned, but gather the wheat into my granary."'"

The Mustard Seed

Matthew 13:31–32

KJV—31 Another parable put he forth unto them, saying, "The kingdom of heaven is like to a grain of mustard seed, which a man took and sowed in his field. 32 Which, indeed, is the least of all seeds, but when it is grown, it is the greatest among herbs and becometh a tree so that the birds of the air come and lodge in the branches thereof."

Amp—31 Another story by way of comparison he set forth before them, saying, "The kingdom of heaven is like a grain of mustard seed, which a man took and sowed in his field. 32 Of all the seeds, it is the smallest, but when it has grown, it is the largest of the garden herbs and becomes a tree so that the birds of the air come and find shelter in its branches."

THE YEAST

Matthew 13:33–43

KJV—33 Another parable spake he unto them: "The kingdom of heaven is like unto leaven, which a woman took and hid in three measures of meal till the whole was leavened." 34 All these things spake Jesus unto the multitude in parables, and without a parable spake he not unto them 35 that it might be fulfilled which was spoken by the prophet, saying, "I will open my mouth in parables; I will utter things which have been kept secret from the foundation of the world." 36 Then Jesus sent the multitude away and went into the house, and his disciples came unto him, saying, "Declare unto us the parable of the tares of the field." 37 He answered and said unto them, "He that soweth the good seed is the Son of man; 38 the field is the world; the good seed are the children of the kingdom, but the tares are the children of the wicked one; 39 the enemy that sowed them is the devil; the harvest is the end of the world; and the reapers are the angels. 40 As, therefore, the tares are gathered and burned in the fire, so shall it be in the end of this world. 41 The Son of man shall send forth his angels, and they shall gather out of his kingdom all things that offend and them which do iniquity 42 and shall cast them into a furnace of fire; there shall be wailing and gnashing of teeth. 43 Then shall the righteous shine forth as the sun in the kingdom of their Father. Who hath ears to hear, let him hear."

Amp—33 He told them another parable: "The kingdom of heaven is like leaven sour dough, which a woman took and covered over in three measures of meal or flour till all of it was leavened." 34 These things, all taken together, Jesus said to the crowds in parables; indeed, without a parable, he said nothing to them. 35 This was in fulfillment of what was spoken by the prophet: "I will open my mouth in parables; I will utter things that have been hidden since the foundation of the world." 36 Then he left the throngs and went into the house. And his disciples came to him, saying, "Explain to us the parable of the darnel in the field." 37 He answered, "He who sows the good seed is the Son of man. 38 The field is the world, and the good seed means the children of the kingdom; the darnel is the children of the evil one, 39 and the enemy who sowed it is the devil. The harvest is the close and consummation of the age, and the reapers are angels. 40 Just as the darnel weeds resembling wheat is gathered and burned with fire, so it will be at the close of the age. 41 The Son of man will send forth his angels, and they will gather out of his kingdom all causes of offense, persons by whom others are drawn into error or sin and all who do iniquity and act wickedly, 42 and will cast them into the furnace of fire; there will be weeping and wailing and grinding of teeth. 43 Then will the righteous those who are upright and in right standing with God shine forth like the sun in the kingdom of their Father. Let him who has ears to hear be listening, and let him consider and perceive and understand by hearing."

HIDDEN TREASURE

Matthew 13:44

— ❧ —

KJV—44 Again, the kingdom of heaven is like unto treasure hid in a field; the which when a man hath found, he hideth and for joy thereof goeth and selleth all that he hath and buyeth that field.

Amp—44 The kingdom of heaven is like something precious buried in a field, which a man found and hid again; then in his joy, he goes and sells all he has and buys that field.

The Pearl

Matthew 13:45–46

―――――――――― ⧏⧐ ――――――――――

KJV—45 Again, the kingdom of heaven is like unto a merchant man seeking goodly pearls, 46 who, when he had found one pearl of great price, went and sold all that he had and bought it.

Amp—45 Again, the kingdom of heaven is like a man who is a dealer in search of fine and precious pearls, 46 who, on finding a single pearl of great price, went and sold all he had and bought it.

THE NET

Matthew 13:47–50

—✦—

KJV—47 Again, the kingdom of heaven is like unto a net that was cast into the sea and gathered of every kind, 48 which, when it was full, they drew to shore and sat down and gathered the good into vessels but cast the bad away. 49 So shall it be at the end of the world: the angels shall come forth and sever the wicked from among the just 50 and shall cast them into the furnace of fire; there shall be wailing and gnashing of teeth.

Amp—47 Again, the kingdom of heaven is like a dragnet which was cast into the sea and gathered in fish of every sort. 48 When it was full, men dragged it up on the beach and sat down and sorted out the good fish into baskets, but the worthless ones they threw away. 49 So it will be at the close and consummation of the age. The angels will go forth and separate the wicked from the righteous, those who are upright and in right standing with God, 50 and cast them, the wicked, into the furnace of fire; there will be weeping and wailing and grinding of teeth.

HOUSEHOLDER

Matthew 13:52

KJV—52 Then said he unto them, "Therefore every scribe which is instructed unto the kingdom of heaven is like unto a man that is an householder, which bringeth forth out of his treasure things new and old."

Amp—52 He said to them, "Therefore every teacher and interpreter of the sacred writings, who has been instructed about and trained for the kingdom of heaven and has become a disciple, is like a householder who brings forth out of his storehouse treasure that is new and treasure that is old, the fresh as well as the familiar."

The Lost Sheep

Matthew 18:12–14

KJV—12 How think ye? If a man have an hundred sheep, and one of them be gone astray, doth he not leave the ninety and nine and goeth into the mountains and seeketh that which is gone astray? 13 And if so be that he find it, verily I say unto you, he rejoiceth more of that sheep than of the ninety and nine which went not astray. 14 Even so, it is not the will of your Father, which is in heaven, that one of these little ones should perish.

Amp—12 What do you think? If a man has a hundred sheep, and one of them has gone astray and gets lost, will he not leave the ninety-nine on the mountain and go in search of the one that is lost? 13 And if it should be that he finds it, truly I say to you, he rejoices more over it than over the ninety-nine that did not get lost. 14 Just so it is not the will of my Father who is in heaven that one of these little ones should be lost and perish.

The Unmerciful Servant

Matthew 18:23–35

———— ❦ ————

KJV—23 Therefore is the kingdom of heaven likened unto a certain king, which would take account of his servants. 24 And when he had begun to reckon, one was brought unto him, which owed him ten thousand talents. 25 But forasmuch as he had not to pay, his lord commanded him to be sold, and his wife and children and all that he had, and payment to be made. 26 The servant, therefore, fell down and worshipped him, saying, "Lord, have patience with me, and I will pay thee all." 27 Then the lord of that servant was moved with compassion and loosed him and forgave him the debt. 28 But the same servant went out and found one of his fellowservants, which owed him an hundred pence, and he laid hands on him and took him by the throat, saying, "Pay me that thou owest." 29 And his fellowservant fell down at his feet and besought him, saying, "Have patience with me, and I will pay thee all." 30 And he would not but went and cast him into prison till he should pay the debt. 31 So when his fellowservants saw what was done, they were very sorry and came and told unto their lord all that was done. 32 Then his lord, after that he had called him, said unto him, "O thou wicked servant, I forgave thee all that debt because thou desiredst me; 33 shouldest not thou also have had compassion on thy fellowservant, even as I had pity on thee?" 34 And his lord was wroth and delivered him to the tormentors till he should pay all that was due unto him. 35 So likewise shall my heavenly Father do also unto you if ye from your hearts forgive not every one his brother their trespasses.

Amp—23 Therefore the kingdom of heaven is like a human king who wished to settle accounts with his attendants. 24 When he began the accounting, one was brought to him who owed him 10,000 talents, (probably about $10,000,000). 25 And because he could not pay, his master ordered him to be sold, with his wife and his children and everything that he possessed, and payment to be made. 26 So the attendant fell on his knees, begging him, "Have patience with me, and I will pay you everything." 27 And his master's heart was moved with compassion, and he released him and forgave him, cancelling the debt. 28 But that same attendant, as he went out, found one of his fellow attendants who owed him a hundred denarii, about twenty dollars, and he caught him by the throat and said, "Pay what you owe." 29 So his fellow attendant fell down and begged him earnestly, "Give me time, and I will pay you all." 30 But he was unwilling, and he went out and had him put in prison till he should pay the debt. 31 When his fellow attendants saw what had happened, they were greatly distressed, and they went and told everything that had taken place to their master. 32 Then his master called him and said to him, "You contemptible and wicked attendant! I forgave and cancelled all that great debt of yours because you begged me to. 33 And should you not have had pity and mercy on your fellow attendant, as I had pity and mercy on you?" 34

And in wrath, his master turned him over to the torturers, the jailers, till he should pay all that he owed. 35 So also my heavenly Father will deal with every one of you if you do not freely forgive your brother from your heart his offenses.

The Workers in the Vineyard

Matthew 20:1–16

———— ⚬ ————

KJV—1 For the kingdom of heaven is like unto a man that is an householder, which went out early in the morning to hire labourers into his vineyard. 2 And when he had agreed with the labourers for a penny a day, he sent them into his vineyard. 3 And he went out about the third hour and saw others standing idle in the marketplace 4 and said unto them, "Go ye also into the vineyard, and whatsoever is right, I will give you." And they went their way. 5 Again he went out about the sixth and ninth hour and did likewise. 6 And about the eleventh hour, he went out and found others standing idle and saith unto them, "Why stand ye here all the day idle?" 7 They say unto him, "Because no man hath hired us." He saith unto them, "Go ye also into the vineyard, and whatsoever is right, that shall ye receive." 8 So when even was come, the lord of the vineyard saith unto his steward, "Call the labourers, and give them their hire, beginning from the last unto the first." 9 And when they came that were hired about the eleventh hour, they received every man a penny. 10 But when the first came, they supposed that they should have received more, and they likewise received every man a penny.

11 And when they had received it, they murmured against the goodman of the house, 12 saying, "These last have wrought but one hour, and thou hast made them equal unto us, which have borne the burden and heat of the day." 13 But he answered one of them and said, "Friend, I do thee no wrong; didst not thou agree with me for a penny? 14 Take that thine is, and go thy way. I will give unto this last, even as unto thee. 15 Is it not lawful for me to do what I will with mine own? Is thine eye evil because I am good? 16 So the last shall be first, and the first last, for many be called, but few chosen."

Amp—1 For the kingdom of heaven is like the owner of an estate who went out in the morning along with the dawn to hire workmen for his vineyard. 2 After agreeing with the laborers for a denarius a day, he sent them into his vineyard. 3 And going out about the third hour, nine o'clock, he saw others standing idle in the marketplace, 4 and he said to them, "You go also into the vineyard, and whatever is right, I will pay you." And they went. 5 He went out again about the sixth hour, noon, and the ninth hour, three o'clock, he did the same. 6 And about the eleventh hour, five o'clock, he went out and found still others standing around and said to them, "Why do you stand here idle all day?" 7 They answered him, "Because nobody has hired us." He told them, "You go out into the vineyard also, and you will get whatever is just and fair." 8 When evening came, the owner of the vineyard said to his manager, "Call the workmen, and pay them their wages, beginning with the last, and ending with the first." 9 And those who had been hired at the eleventh hour, five o'clock, came and received a denarius each. 10 Now when the first came, they supposed they would get more, but each of them also received a denarius. 11 And when they received it, they grumbled at the owner of the estate, 12 saying, "These men who came last worked no more than an hour, and yet you have made them rank with us who have borne the burden and the scorching heat of the day." 13 But he answered one of them, "Friend, I am doing you no injustice. Did you not agree with me for a denarius? 14 Take what belongs to you, and go. I choose to give to this man hired last the same as I give to you. 15 Am I not permitted to do what I choose with what is mine? Or do you begrudge my being generous? Is your eye evil because I am good? 16 So those who now are last will be first then, and those who now are first will be last then. For many are called, but few chosen."

THE TWO SONS

Matthew 21:28–32

KJV—28 But what think ye? A certain man had two sons, and he came to the first, and said, "Son, go work to day in my vineyard." 29 He answered and said, "I will not," but afterward he repented and went. 30 And he came to the second and said likewise. And he answered and said, "I go, sir," and went not. 31 Whether of them twain did the will of his father? They say unto him, "the first." Jesus saith unto them, "Verily I say unto you that the publicans and the harlots go into the kingdom of God before you. 32 For John came unto you in the way of righteousness, and ye believed him not, but the publicans and the harlots believed him, and ye, when ye had seen it, repented not afterward that ye might believe him."

Amp—28 What do you think? There was a man who had two sons. He came to the first and said, "Son, go and work today in the vineyard." 29 And he answered, "I will not," but afterward he changed his mind and went. 30 Then the man came to the second and said the same thing. And he replied, "I will go, sir," but he did not go. 31 Which of the two did the will of the father?

They replied, "the first one." Jesus said to them, "Truly I tell you, the tax collectors and the harlots will get into the kingdom of heaven before you. 32 For John came to you, walking in the way of an upright man in right standing with God, and you did not believe him, but the tax collectors and the harlots did believe him, and you, even when you saw that, did not afterward change your minds and believe him adhere to, trust in, and rely on what he told you."

THE TENANTS

Matthew 21:33–41

———————— ❧ ————————

KJV—33 Hear another parable: There was a certain householder, which planted a vineyard and hedged it round about and digged a winepress in it and built a tower and let it out to husbandmen and went into a far country. 34 And when the time of the fruit drew near, he sent his servants to the husbandmen that they might receive the fruits of it. 35 And the husbandmen took his servants and beat one and killed another and stoned another. 36 Again, he sent other servants more than the first, and they did unto them likewise. 37 But last of all, he sent unto them his son, saying, "They will reverence my son." 38 But when the husbandmen saw the son, they said among themselves, "This is the heir; come, let us kill him, and let us seize on his inheritance." 39 And they caught him and cast him out of the vineyard and slew him. 40 When the lord therefore of the vineyard cometh, what will he do unto those husbandmen? 41 They say unto him, "He will miserably destroy those wicked men and will let out his vineyard unto other husbandmen, which shall render him the fruits in their seasons."

Amp—33 Listen to another parable: There was a master of a house who planted a vineyard and put a hedge around it and dug a wine vat in it and built a watchtower. Then he let it out for rent to tenants and went into another country. 34 When the fruit season drew near, he sent his servants to the tenants to get his share of the fruit. 35 But the tenants took his servants and beat one, killed another, and stoned another. 36 Again he sent other servants, more than the first time, and they treated them the same way. 37 Finally he sent his own son to them, saying, "They will respect and give heed to my son." 38 But when the tenants saw the son, they said to themselves, "This is the heir; come on, let us kill him and have his inheritance." 39 And they took him and threw him out of the vineyard and killed him. 40 Now when the owner of the vineyard comes back, what will he do to those tenants? 41 They said to him, "He will put those wretches to a miserable death and rent the vineyard to other tenants of such a character that they will give him the fruits promptly in their season."

The Wedding Banquet

Matthew 22:1–14

—⁂—

KJV—1 And Jesus answered and spake unto them again by parables, and said, 2 "The kingdom of heaven is like unto a certain king, which made a marriage for his son 3 and sent forth his servants to call them that were bidden to the wedding, and they would not come. 4 Again he sent forth other servants, saying, 'Tell them which are bidden, "Behold, I have prepared my dinner: my oxen and my fatlings are killed, and all things are ready; come unto the marriage."' 5 But they made light of it and went their ways, one to his farm, another to his merchandise, 6 and the remnant took his servants and entreated them spitefully and slew them. 7 But when the king heard thereof, he was wroth, and he sent forth his armies and destroyed those murderers and burned up their city. 8 Then saith he to his servants, 'The wedding is ready, but they which were bidden were not worthy. 9 Go ye therefore into the highways, and as many as ye shall find, bid to the marriage.' 10 So those servants went out into the highways and gathered together all as many as they found, both bad and good, and the wedding was furnished with guests. 11 And when the king came in to see the guests, he saw there a man which had not on a wedding garment, 12 And he saith unto him, 'Friend, how camest thou in hither not having a wedding garment?' And he was speechless. 13 Then said the king to the servants, 'Bind him, hand and foot, and take him away, and cast him into outer darkness; there shall be weeping and gnashing of teeth. 14 For many are called, but few are chosen.'"

Amp—1 And again Jesus spoke to them in parables, comparisons, stories used to illustrate and explain, saying, 2 "The kingdom of heaven is like a king who gave a wedding banquet for his son 3 and sent his servants to summon those who had been invited to the wedding banquet, but they refused to come. 4 Again he sent other servants, saying, 'Tell those who are invited, "Behold, I have prepared my banquet; my bullocks and my fat calves are killed, and everything is prepared; come to the wedding feast."' 5 But they were not concerned and paid no attention; they ignored and made light of the summons, treating it with contempt, and they went away—one to his farm, another to his business. 6 While the others seized his servants, treated them shamefully, and put them to death. 7 Hearing this, the king was infuriated, and he sent his soldiers and put those murderers to death and burned their city. 8 Then he said to his servants, 'The wedding feast is prepared, but those invited were not worthy. 9 So go to the thoroughfares where they leave the city where the main roads and those from the country end, and invite to the wedding feast as many as you find.' 10 And those servants went out on the crossroads and got together as many as they found, both bad and good, so [the room in which] the wedding feast was held was filled with guests. 11 But when the king came in to view the guests, he looked intently at a man there who had on no wedding garment. 12 And he said, 'Friend, how did you come in here without putting on the appropriate wedding garment?' And he was speechless, muzzled, gagged. 13 Then the king said to the attendants, 'Tie him, hand and foot, and throw him into the darkness outside; there will be weeping and grinding of teeth. 14 For many are called invited and summoned, but few are chosen.'"

THE DOOR KEEPER

Matthew 24:42–44

KJV—42 Watch, therefore, for ye know not what hour your Lord doth come. 43 But know this, that if the goodman of the house had known in what watch the thief would come, he would have watched and would not have suffered his house to be broken up. 44 Therefore, be ye also ready, for in such an hour as ye think not the Son of man cometh.

Amp—42 Watch, therefore, give strict attention, be cautious and active, for you do not know in what kind of a day whether a near or remote one your Lord is coming. 43 But understand this: had the householder known in what part of the night, whether in a night or a morning watch the thief was coming, he would have watched and would not have allowed his house to be undermined and broken into. 44 You also must be ready therefore, for the Son of man is coming at an hour when you do not expect him.

The Faithful and Wise Servant

Matthew 24:45–51

———— ✗ ————

KJV—45 Who then is a faithful and wise servant, whom his lord hath made ruler over his household, to give them meat in due season? 46 Blessed is that servant, whom his lord, when he cometh, shall find so doing. 47 Verily I say unto you that he shall make him ruler over all his goods. 48 But and if that evil servant shall say in his heart, "My lord delayeth his coming," 49 and shall begin to smite his fellow servants and to eat and drink with the drunken, 50 the lord of that servant shall come in a day when he looketh not for him and in an hour that he is not aware of 51 and shall cut him asunder and appoint him his portion with the hypocrites; there shall be weeping and gnashing of teeth.

Amp—45 Who then is the faithful, thoughtful, and wise servant, whom his master has put in charge of his household to give to the others the food and supplies at the proper time? 46 Blessed happy, fortunate, and to be envied is that servant whom, when his master comes, he will find so doing. 47 I solemnly declare to you, he will set him over all his possessions. 48 But if that servant is wicked and says to himself, "My master is delayed and is going to be gone a long time," 49 and begins to beat his fellow servants and to eat and drink with the drunken, 50 the master of that servant will come on a day when he does not expect him and at an hour of which he is not aware 51 and will punish him [cut him up by scourging] and put him with the pretenders, hypocrites; there will be weeping and grinding of teeth.

THE TEN VIRGINS

Matthew 25:1–13

———— ❧ ————

KJV—1 Then shall the kingdom of heaven be likened unto ten virgins, which took their lamps and went forth to meet the bridegroom. 2 And five of them were wise, and five were foolish. 3 They that were foolish took their lamps and took no oil with them, 4 but the wise took oil in their vessels with their lamps. 5 While the bridegroom tarried, they all slumbered and slept. 6 And at midnight, there was a cry made, "Behold, the bridegroom cometh; go ye out to meet him." 7 Then all those virgins arose and trimmed their lamps. 8 And the foolish said unto the wise, "Give us of your oil, for our lamps are gone out." 9 But the wise answered, saying, "Not so, lest there be not enough for us and you, but go ye rather to them that sell, and buy for yourselves." 10 And while they went to buy, the bridegroom came, and they that were ready went in with him to the marriage, and the door was shut. 11 Afterward came also the other virgins, saying, "Lord, Lord, open to us." 12 But he answered and said, "Verily I say unto you, I know you not." 13 Watch, therefore, for ye know neither the day nor the hour wherein the Son of man cometh.

Amp—1 Then the kingdom of heaven shall be likened to ten virgins who took their lamps and went to meet the bridegroom.

2 Five of them were foolish, thoughtless, without forethought, and five were wise, sensible, intelligent, and prudent. 3 For when the foolish took their lamps, they did not take any extra oil with them. 4 But the wise took flasks of oil along with them also with their lamps. 5 While the bridegroom lingered and was slow in coming, they all began nodding their heads, and they fell asleep. 6 But at midnight, there was a shout, "Behold, the bridegroom! Go out to meet him!" 7 Then all those virgins got up and put their own lamps in order. 8 And the foolish said to the wise, "Give us some of your oil, for our lamps are going out." 9 But the wise replied, "There will not be enough for us and for you; go instead to the dealers, and buy for yourselves." 10 But while they were going away to buy, the bridegroom came, and those who were prepared went in with him to the marriage feast, and the door was shut. 11 Later the other virgins also came and said, "Lord, Lord, open the door to us!" 12 But he replied, "I solemnly declare to you, I do not know you. I am not acquainted with you." 13 Watch, therefore, give strict attention, and be cautious and active, for you know neither the day nor the hour when the Son of man will come.

The Talents

Matthew 25:14–30

———— ❦ ————

KJV—14 For the kingdom of heaven is as a man travelling into a far country, who called his own servants and delivered unto them his goods. 15 And unto one he gave five talents, to another two, and to another one—to every man according to his several ability—and straightway took his journey. 16 Then he that had received the five talents went and traded with the same and made them other five talents. 17 And likewise he that had received two, he also gained other two. 18 But he that had received one went and digged in the earth, and hid his lord's money. 19 After a long time, the lord of those servants cometh, and reckoneth with them. 20 And so he that had received five talents came and brought other five talents, saying, "Lord, thou deliveredst unto me five talents; behold, I have gained beside them five talents more." 21 His lord said unto him, "Well done, thou good and faithful servant; thou hast been faithful over a few things. I will make thee ruler over many things; enter thou into the joy of thy lord." 22 He also that had received two talents came and said, "Lord, thou deliveredst unto me two talents; behold, I have gained two other talents beside them." 23 His lord said unto him, "Well done, good and faithful servant; thou hast been faithful over a few things. I will make thee ruler over many things; enter thou into the joy of thy lord." 24 Then he which had received the one talent came and said, "Lord, I knew thee that thou art an hard man, reaping where thou hast not sown and gathering where thou hast not strawed. 25 And I was afraid and went and hid thy talent in the earth; lo, there thou hast that is thine." 26 His lord answered and said unto him, "Thou wicked and slothful servant, thou knewest that I reap where I sowed not and gather where I have not strawed. 27 Thou oughtest therefore to have put my money to the exchangers, and then at my coming, I should have received mine own with usury. 28 Take therefore the talent from him, and give it unto him which hath ten talents. 29 For unto every one that hath shall be given, and he shall have abundance, but from him that hath not shall be taken away even that which he hath. 30 And cast ye the unprofitable servant into outer darkness; there shall be weeping and gnashing of teeth."

Amp—14 For it is like a man who was about to take a long journey, and he called his servants together and entrusted them with his property. 15 To one he gave five talents, (probably about $5,000,) to another two, to another one, to each in proportion to his own personal ability. Then he departed and left the country. 16 He who had received the five talents went at once and traded with them, and he gained five talents more. 17 And likewise, he who had received the two talents, he also gained two talents more. 18 But he who had received the one talent went and dug a hole in the ground and hid his master's money. 19 Now after a long time, the master of those servants returned and settled accounts with them. 20 And he who had received the five talents came and brought him five more, saying, "Master, you entrusted to me five talents; see, here I have gained five talents more." 21 His master said to him, "Well done, you upright, honorable, admirable, and faithful servant! You have been faithful and trustworthy over a little; I will put you in charge of much. Enter into and share the joy, the delight, the blessedness which your master enjoys." 22 And he also who had the two talents came forward, saying, "Master, you entrusted two talents to me; here I have gained two talents more." 23 His master said to him, "Well done, you upright, honorable, admirable, and faithful servant! You have been faithful and trustworthy over a little; I will put you in charge of much. Enter into and share the joy, the delight, the blessedness which your master enjoys." 24 He who had received one talent also came forward, saying, "Master, I knew you to be a harsh and hard man, reaping where you did not sow and gathering where you had not winnowed the grain. 25 So I was afraid, and I went and hid your talent in the ground. Here you have what is your own." 26 But his master answered him, "You wicked and lazy and idle servant! Did you, indeed, know that I reap where I have not sowed and gather grain where I have not winnowed? 27 Then you should have invested my money with the bankers, and at my coming, I would have received what was my own with interest. 28 So take the talent away from him, and give it to the one who has the ten talents. 29 For to everyone who has will more be given, and he will be furnished richly so that he will have an abundance, but from the one who does not have, even what he does have will be taken away. 30 And throw the good-for-nothing servant into the outer darkness; there will be weeping and grinding of teeth."

He answered and said unto them, "Because it is given unto you to know the mysteries of the kingdom of heaven, but to them it is not given." Matthew 13:11

THE DIVIDED KINGDOM

Mark 3:23–27

———————— ⚉ ————————

KJV—23 And he called them unto him and said unto them in parables, "How can Satan cast out Satan? 24 And if a kingdom be divided against itself, that kingdom cannot stand. 25 And if a house be divided against itself, that house cannot stand. 26 And if Satan rise up against himself and be divided, he cannot stand but hath an end. 27 No man can enter into a strong man's house and spoil his goods, except he will first bind the strong man, and then he will spoil his house."

Amp—23 And he summoned them to him and said to them in parables, illustrations, or comparisons put beside truths to explain them, "How can Satan drive out Satan? 24 And if a kingdom is divided and rebelling against itself, that kingdom cannot stand. 25 And if a house is divided, split into factions, and rebelling against itself, that house will not be able to last. 26 And if Satan has raised an insurrection against himself and is divided, he cannot stand but is surely coming to an end. 27 But no one can go into a strong man's house and ransack his household goods right and left and seize them as plunder unless he first binds the strong man; then, indeed, he may thoroughly plunder his house."

THE SOWER

Mark 4:2–20

KJV—2 And he taught them many things by parables, and said unto them in his doctrine, 3 "Hearken; behold, there went out a sower to sow, 4 and it came to pass, as he sowed, some fell by the way side, and the fowls of the air came and devoured it up. 5 And some fell on stony ground, where it had not much earth, and immediately it sprang up, because it had no depth of earth. 6 But when the sun was up, it was scorched, and because it had no root, it withered away. 7 And some fell among thorns, and the thorns grew up and choked it, and it yielded no fruit. 8 And other fell on good ground and did yield fruit that sprang up and increased and brought forth some thirty and some sixty and some an hundred." 9 And he said unto them, "He that hath ears to hear, let him hear." 10 And when he was alone, they that were about him with the twelve asked of him the parable. 11 And he said unto them, "Unto you it is given to know the mystery of the kingdom of God, but unto them that are without, all these things are done in parables. 12 That seeing they may see and not perceive, and hearing they may hear and not understand, lest at any time they should be converted and their sins should be forgiven them." 13 And he said unto them, "Know ye not this parable? And how then will ye know all parables? 14 The sower soweth the word. 15 And these are they by the way side, where the word is sown, but when they have heard, Satan cometh immediately and taketh away the word that was sown in their hearts. 16 And these are they, likewise which are sown on stony ground, who, when they have heard the word, immediately receive it with gladness 17 and have no root in themselves and so endure but for a time; afterward, when affliction or persecution ariseth for the word's sake, immediately they are offended. 18 And these are they which are sown among thorns, such as hear the word 19 and the cares of this world and the deceitfulness of riches and the lusts of other things entering in, choke the word, and it becometh unfruitful. 20 And these are they which are sown on good ground, such as hear the word and receive it and bring forth fruit, some thirtyfold, some sixty, and some an hundred."

Amp—2 And he taught them many things in parables, illustrations or comparisons put beside truths to explain them, and in his teaching, he said to them: 3 "Give attention to this! Behold, a sower went out to sow. 4 And as he was sowing, some seed fell along the path, and the birds came and ate it up. 5 Other seed of the same kind fell on ground full of rocks, where it had not much soil, and at once it sprang up because it had no depth of soil. 6 And when the sun came up, it was scorched, and because it had not taken root, it withered away. 7 Other seed of the same kind fell among thorn plants, and the thistles grew and pressed together and utterly choked and suffocated it, and it yielded no grain. 8 And other seed of the same kind fell into good well-adapted soil and brought forth grain, growing up and increasing and yielded up to thirty times as much, and sixty times as much, and even a hundred times as much as had been sown." 9 And he said, "He who has ears to hear, let him be hearing and let him consider, and comprehend." 10 And as soon as he was alone, those who were around him, with the twelve apostles, began to ask him about the parables. 11 And he said to them, "To you has been entrusted the mystery of the kingdom of God, that is, the secret counsels of God which are hidden from the ungodly, but for those outside of our circle, everything becomes a parable 12 in order that they may, indeed, look and look but not see and perceive and may hear and hear but not grasp and comprehend, lest haply they should turn again, and it their willful rejection of the truth should be forgiven them." 13 And he said to them, "Do you not discern and understand this parable? How then is it possible for you to discern and understand all the parables? 14 The sower sows the word. 15 The ones along the path are those who have the word sown in their hearts, but when they hear, Satan comes at once and, by force, takes away the message which is sown in them. 16 And in the same way, the ones sown upon stony ground are those who, when they hear the word, at once receive and accept and welcome it with joy. 17 And they have no real root in themselves, and so they endure for a little while; then when trouble or persecution arises on account of the word, they immediately are offended, become displeased, indignant, resentful, and they stumble and fall away. 18 And the ones sown among the thorns are others who hear the word; 19 then the cares and anxieties of the world and distractions of the age and the pleasure and delight and false glamour and deceitfulness of riches and the craving and passionate desire for other things creep in and choke and suffocate the word, and it becomes fruitless. 20

And those sown on the good well-adapted soil are the ones who hear the word and receive and accept and welcome it and bear fruit some thirty times as much as was sown, some sixty times as much, and some even a hundred times as much."

GROWING SEED

Mark 4:26–29

KJV—26 And he said, "So is the kingdom of God, as if a man should cast seed into the ground 27 and should sleep and rise, night and day, and the seed should spring and grow up, he knoweth not how. 28 For the earth bringeth forth fruit of herself: first the blade, then the ear, after that the full corn in the ear. 29 But when the fruit is brought forth, immediately he putteth in the sickle, because the harvest is come."

Amp—26 And he said, "The kingdom of God is like a man who scatters seed upon the ground 27 and then continues sleeping and rising, night and day, while the seed sprouts and grows and increases, he knows not how. 28 The earth produces, acting by itself, first the blade, then the ear, then the full grain in the ear. 29 But when the grain is ripe and permits, immediately he sends forth the reapers and puts in the sickle, because the harvest stands ready."

THE MUSTARD SEED

Mark 4:30–32

KJV—30 And he said, "Whereunto shall we liken the kingdom of God? Or with what comparison shall we compare it? 31 It is like a grain of mustard seed, which, when it is sown in the earth, is less than all the seeds that be in the earth. 32 But when it is sown, it groweth up and becometh greater than all herbs and shooteth out great branches so that the fowls of the air may lodge under the shadow of it."

Amp—30 And he said, "With what can we compare the kingdom of God, or what parable shall we use to illustrate and explain it? 31 It is like a grain of mustard seed, which, when sown upon the ground, is the smallest of all seeds upon the earth. 32 Yet after it is sown, it grows up and becomes the greatest of all garden herbs and puts out large branches so that the birds of the air are able to make nests and dwell in its shade."

The Clean and Unclean

Mark 7:14–23

———— ❦ ————

KJV—14 And when he had called all the people unto him, he said unto them, "Hearken unto me every one of you, and understand: 15 there is nothing from without a man that entering into him can defile him, but the things which come out of him, those are they that defile the man. 16 If any man have ears to hear, let him hear." 17 And when he was entered into the house from the people, his disciples asked him concerning the parable. 18 And he saith unto them, "Are ye so without understanding also? Do ye not perceive that, whatsoever thing from without entereth into the man, it cannot defile him. 19 Because it entereth not into his heart but into the belly and goeth out into the draught, purging all meats?" 20 And he said, "That which cometh out of the man, that defileth the man. 21 For from within, out of the heart of men, proceed evil thoughts, adulteries, fornications, murders, 22 thefts, covetousness, wickedness, deceit, lasciviousness, an evil eye, blasphemy, pride, foolishness. 23 All these evil things come from within and defile the man."

Amp—14 And he called the people to him again and said to them, "Listen to me, all of you, and understand what I say. 15 There is not even one thing outside a man which by going into him can pollute and defile him, but the things which come out of a man are what defile him and make him unhallowed and unclean. 16 If any man has ears to hear, let him be listening and let him perceive and comprehend by hearing." 17 And when he had left the crowd and had gone into the house, his disciples began asking him about the parable. 18 And he said to them, "Then are you also unintelligent and dull and without understanding? Do you not discern and see that whatever goes into a man from the outside cannot make him unhallowed or unclean 19 since it does not reach and enter his heart but only his digestive tract and so passes on into the place designed to receive waste?" Thus he was making and declaring all foods ceremonially clean; that is, abolishing the ceremonial distinctions of the Levitical Law. 20 And he said, "What comes out of a man is what makes a man unclean and renders him unhallowed. 21 For from within, that is out of the hearts of men, come base and wicked thoughts, sexual immorality, stealing, murder, adultery, 22 coveting, greedy desire to have more wealth, dangerous and destructive wickedness, deceit, unrestrained indecent conduct, an evil eye envy, slander, evil speaking, malicious misrepresentation, abusiveness, pride, the sin of an uplifted heart against God and man, foolishness, folly, lack of sense, recklessness, thoughtlessness. 23 All these evil purposes and desires come from within, and they make the man unclean and render him unhallowed."

THE TENANTS

Mark 12:1–11

———— ❧ ————

KJV—1 And he began to speak unto them by parables. A certain man planted a vineyard and set an hedge about it and digged a place for the winefat and built a tower and let it out to husbandmen and went into a far country. 2 And at the season, he sent to the husbandmen a servant, that he might receive from the husbandmen of the fruit of the vineyard. 3 And they caught him and beat him and sent him away empty. 4 And again he sent unto them another servant, and at him, they cast stones and wounded him in the head and sent him away shamefully handled. 5 And again he sent another, and him they killed, and many others—beating some and killing some. 6 Having yet therefore one son, his well beloved, he sent him also last unto them, saying, "They will reverence my son." 7 But those husbandmen said among themselves, "This is the heir; come, let us kill him, and the inheritance shall be ours." 8 And they took him and killed him and cast him out of the vineyard. 9 What shall, therefore, the lord of the vineyard do? He will come and destroy the husbandmen and will give the vineyard unto others. 10 And have ye not read this scripture; the stone which the builders rejected is become the head of the corner. 11 This was the Lord's doing, and it is marvellous in our eyes?

Amp—1 And Jesus started to speak to them in parables with comparisons and illustrations. A man planted a vineyard and put a hedge around it and dug a pit for the winepress and built a tower and let it out for rent to vinedressers and went into another country. 2 When the season came, he sent a bond servant to the tenants to collect from them some of the fruit of the vineyard. 3 But they took him and beat him and sent him away without anything. 4 Again he sent to them another bond servant, and they stoned him and wounded him in the head and treated him shamefully, sending him away with insults. 5 And he sent another, and that one they killed, then many others—some they beat, and some they put to death. 6 He had still one left to send, a beloved son; last of all, he sent him to them, saying, "They will respect my son." 7 But those tenants said to one another, "Here is the heir; come on, let us put him to death, and then the inheritance will be ours." 8 And they took him and killed him and threw his body outside the vineyard. 9 Now what will the owner of the vineyard do? He will come and destroy the tenants and give the vineyard to others. 10 Have you not even read this passage of scripture: The very stone which after putting it to the test the builders rejected has become the head of the corner cornerstone. 11 This is from the Lord and is his doing, and it is marvelous in our eyes?

THE DAY AND HOUR UNKNOWN

Mark 13:34–37

———— ❦ ————

KJV—34 For the Son of man is as a man taking a far journey, who left his house and gave authority to his servants and to every man his work and commanded the porter to watch. 35 Watch ye therefore, for ye know not when the master of the house cometh at even or at midnight or at the cockcrowing or in the morning: 36 Lest coming suddenly he find you sleeping. 37 And what I say unto you I say unto all: watch.

Amp—34 It is like a man already going on a journey; when he leaves home, he puts his servants in charge, each with his particular task, and he gives orders to the doorkeeper to be constantly alert and on the watch. 35 Therefore, watch, give strict attention, be cautious and alert, for you do not know when the master of the house is coming in the evening or at midnight or at cockcrowing or in the morning. 36 Watch, I say lest he come suddenly and unexpectedly and find you asleep. 37 And what I say to you I say to everybody: watch, give strict attention, be cautious, active, and alert.

And he said unto them, "Unto you it is given to know the mystery of the kingdom of God, but unto them that are without, all these things are done in parables." Mark 4:11

THE NEW GARMENT

Luke 5:36

KJV—36 And he spake also a parable unto them: No man putteth a piece of a new garment upon an old; if otherwise, then both the new maketh a rent, and the piece that was taken out of the new agreeth not with the old.

Amp—36 He told them a proverb also: No one puts a patch from a new garment on an old garment; if he does, he will both tear the new one, and the patch from the new one will not match the old garment.

The New Wine

Luke 5:37

— ❧ —

KJV—37 And no man putteth new wine into old bottles, else the new wine will burst the bottles and be spilled, and the bottles shall perish. 38 But new wine must be put into new bottles, and both are preserved.

Amp—37 And no one pours new wine into old wineskins; if he does, the fresh wine will burst the skins, and it will be spilled, and the skins will be ruined destroyed. 38 But new wine must be put into fresh wineskins.

The Old Wine

Luke 5:39

—❦—

KJV—39 No man also having drunk old wine straightway desireth new, for he saith, "The old is better."

Amp—39 And no one, after drinking old wine, immediately desires new wine, for he says, "The old is good or better."

The Wise and Foolish Builder

Luke 6:46–49

—❧—

KJV—46 And why call ye me Lord, Lord and do not the things which I say? 47 Whosoever cometh to me and heareth my sayings and doeth them, I will shew you to whom he is like. 48 He is like a man which built an house and digged deep and laid the foundation on a rock, and when the flood arose, the stream beat vehemently upon that house and could not shake it, for it was founded upon a rock. 49 But he that heareth and doeth not is like a man that, without a foundation, built an house upon the earth, against which the stream did beat vehemently, and immediately it fell, and the ruin of that house was great.

Amp—46 Why do you call me Lord, Lord and do not practice what I tell you? 47 For everyone who comes to me and listens to my words in order to heed their teaching and does them, I will show you what he is like: 48 he is like a man building a house, who dug and went down deep and laid a foundation upon the rock, and when a flood arose, the torrent broke against that house and could not shake or move it because it had been securely built or founded on a rock. 49 But he who merely hears and does not practice doing my words is like a man who built a house on the ground without a foundation, against which the torrent burst, and immediately it collapsed and fell, and the breaking and ruin of that house was great.

The Two Debtors

Luke 7:41–43

———— ⸎ ————

KJV—41 There was a certain creditor which had two debtors: the one owed five hundred pence and the other fifty. 42 And when they had nothing to pay, he frankly forgave them both. Tell me, therefore, which of them will love him most? 43 Simon answered and said, "I suppose that he, to whom he forgave most." And he said unto him, "Thou hast rightly judged."

Amp—41 A certain lender of money at interest had two debtors: one owed him five hundred denarii and the other fifty. 42 When they had no means of paying, he freely forgave them both. Now which of them will love him more? 43 Simon answered, "The one, I take it, for whom he forgave and cancelled more." And Jesus said to him, "You have decided correctly."

The Sower

Luke 8:5–15

———— ❧ ————

KJV—5 A sower went out to sow his seed, and as he sowed, some fell by the way side, and it was trodden down, and the fowls of the air devoured it. 6 And some fell upon a rock, and as soon as it was sprung up, it withered away because it lacked moisture. 7 And some fell among thorns, and the thorns sprang up with it and choked it. 8 And other fell on good ground and sprang up and bare fruit an hundredfold. And when he had said these things, he cried, "He that hath ears to hear, let him hear." 9 And his disciples asked him, saying, "What might this parable be?" 10 And he said, "Unto you it is given to know the mysteries of the kingdom of God, but to others in parables, that seeing they might not see and hearing they might not understand. 11 Now the parable is this: The seed is the word of God. 12 Those by the way side are they that hear; then cometh the devil and taketh away the word out of their hearts, lest they should believe and be saved. 13 They on the rock are they, which, when they hear, receive the word with joy, and these have no root, which for a while believe and, in time of temptation, fall away. 14 And that which fell among thorns are they, which, when they have heard, go forth and are choked with cares and riches and pleasures of this life and bring no fruit to perfection. 15 But that on the good ground are they, which in an honest and good heart, having heard the word, keep it and bring forth fruit with patience."

Amp—5 A sower went out to sow seed, and as he sowed, some fell along the traveled path and was trodden underfoot, and the birds of the air ate it up. 6 And some seed fell on the rock, and as soon as it sprouted, it withered away because it had no moisture. 7 And other seed fell in the midst of the thorns, and the thorns grew up with it and choked it off. 8 And some seed fell into good soil and grew up and yielded a crop a hundred times as great. As he said these things, he called out, "He who has ears to hear, let him be listening and let him consider and understand by hearing." 9 And when his disciples asked him the meaning of this parable, 10 he said to them, "To you it has been given to come progressively to know to recognize and understand more strongly and clearly the mysteries and secrets of the kingdom of God, but for others they are in parables so that, though looking, they may not see and hearing they may not comprehend. 11 Now the meaning of the parable is this: The seed is the word of God. 12 Those along the traveled road are the people who have heard; then the devil comes and carries away the message out of their hearts that they may not believe, acknowledge, me as their savior and devote themselves to me and be saved here and hereafter. 13 And those upon the rock are the people who, when they hear the word, receive and welcome it with joy, but these have no root. They believe for a while, and in time of trial and temptation, fall away, withdraw, and stand aloof. 14 And as for what fell among the thorns, these are the people who hear, but as they go on their way, they are choked and suffocated with the anxieties and cares and riches and pleasures of life, and their fruit does not ripen—come to maturity and perfection. 15 But as for that seed in the good soil, these are the people who, hearing the word, hold it fast in a just, noble, virtuous, and worthy heart and steadily bring forth fruit with patience."

THE GOOD SAMARITAN

Luke 10:30–37

KJV—30 And Jesus answering, said, "A certain man went down from Jerusalem to Jericho and fell among thieves, which stripped him of his raiment and wounded him and departed, leaving him half dead. 31 And by chance, there came down a certain priest that way, and when he saw him, he passed by on the other side. 32 And likewise a Levite, when he was at the place, came and looked on him and passed by on the other side. 33 But a certain Samaritan, as he journeyed, came where he was, and when he saw him, he had compassion on him 34 and went to him and bound up his wounds, pouring in oil and wine, and set him on his own beast and brought him to an inn and took care of him. 35 And on the morrow when he departed, he took out two pence, and gave them to the host and said unto him, 'Take care of him; and whatsoever thou spendest more, when I come again, I will repay thee.' 36 Which now of these three, thinkest thou, was neighbour unto him that fell among the thieves?" 37 And he said, "He that shewed mercy on him." Then said Jesus unto him, "Go, and do thou likewise."

Amp—30 Jesus, taking him up, replied, "A certain man was going from Jerusalem down to Jericho, and he fell among robbers, who stripped him of his clothes and belongings and beat him and went their way, unconcernedly leaving him half dead, as it happened. 31 Now by coincidence, a certain priest was going down along that road, and when he saw him, he passed by on the other side. 32 A Levite likewise came down to the place and saw him and passed by on the other side of the road. 33 But a certain Samaritan, as he traveled along, came down to where he was, and when he saw him, he was moved with pity and sympathy for him 34 and went to him and dressed his wounds, pouring on them oil and wine. Then he set him on his own beast and brought him to an inn and took care of him. 35 And the next day, he took out two denarii, two day's wages, and gave them to the innkeeper, saying, 'Take care of him, and whatever more you spend, I myself will repay you when I return.' 36 Which of these three do you think proved himself a neighbor to him who fell among the robbers?" 37 He answered, "The one who showed pity and mercy to him." And Jesus said to him, "Go and do likewise."

The Importunate Friend

Luke 11:5–8

———— ⋙ ————

KJV—5 And he said unto them, "Which of you shall have a friend and shall go unto him at midnight and say unto him, 'Friend, lend me three loaves, 6 for a friend of mine in his journey is come to me, and I have nothing to set before him?' 7 And he from within shall answer and say, 'Trouble me not; the door is now shut, and my children are with me in bed. I cannot rise and give thee.' 8 I say unto you, though he will not rise and give him, because he is his friend, yet because of his importunity, he will rise and give him as many as he needeth."

Amp—5 And he said to them, "Which of you who has a friend will go to him at midnight and will say to him, 'Friend, lend me three loaves of bread, 6 for a friend of mine who is on a journey has just come, and I have nothing to put before him.' 7 And he from within will answer, 'Do not disturb me; the door is now closed, and my children are with me in bed. I cannot get up and supply you with anything?' 8 I tell you, although he will not get up and supply him anything because he is his friend, yet because of his shameless persistence and insistence, he will get up and give him as much as he needs."

THE STRONGMAN BOUND

Luke 11:21–22

───────────── ⊰❦⊱ ─────────────

KJV—21 When a strong man armed keepeth his palace, his goods are in peace, 22 but when a stronger than he shall come upon him and overcome him, he taketh from him all his armour wherein he trusted and divideth his spoils.

Amp—21 When the strong man, fully armed, from his courtyard guards his own dwelling, his belongings are undisturbed; his property is at peace and is secure. 22 But when one stronger than he attacks him and conquers him, he robs him of his whole armor on which he had relied and divides up and distributes all his goods as plunder spoil.

THE RICH FOOL

Luke 12:16–21

—❦—

KJV—16 And he spake a parable unto them, saying, "The ground of a certain rich man brought forth plentifully, 17 and he thought within himself, saying, 'What shall I do, because I have no room where to bestow my fruits?' 18 And he said, 'This will I do: I will pull down my barns and build greater, and there will I bestow all my fruits and my goods. 19 And I will say to my soul, "Soul, thou hast much goods laid up for many years; take thine ease, eat, drink, and be merry."' 20 But God said unto him, 'Thou fool, this night thy soul shall be required of thee, then whose shall those things be, which thou hast provided?' 21 So is he that layeth up treasure for himself and is not rich toward God."

Amp—16 Then he told them a parable, saying, "The land of a rich man was fertile and yielded plentifully. 17 And he considered and debated within himself, 'What shall I do? I have no place in which to gather together my harvest.' 18 And he said, 'I will do this: I will pull down my storehouses and build larger ones, and there I will store all my grain or produce and my goods.

19 And I will say to my soul, "Soul, you have many good things laid up, enough for many years. Take your ease; eat, drink, and enjoy yourself merrily."' 20 But God said to him, 'You fool! This very night they, the messengers of God, will demand your soul of you; and all the things that you have prepared, whose will they be?' 21 So it is with the one who continues to lay up and hoard possessions for himself and is not rich in his relation to God— this is how he fares."

THE WATCHERS

Luke 12:35–40

———— ⸎ ————

KJV—35 Let your loins be girded about and your lights burning 36 and ye yourselves like unto men that wait for their lord, when he will return from the wedding that, when he cometh and knocketh, they may open unto him immediately. 37 Blessed are those servants, whom the lord when he cometh shall find watching; verily I say unto you that he shall gird himself and make them to sit down to meat and will come forth and serve them. 38 And if he shall come in the second watch or come in the third watch and find them so, blessed are those servants. 39 And this, know that if the goodman of the house had known what hour the thief would come, he would have watched and not have suffered his house to be broken through. 40 Be ye, therefore, ready also, for the Son of man cometh at an hour when ye think not.

Amp—35 Keep your loins girded and your lamps burning, 36 and be like men who are waiting for their master to return home from the marriage feast so that, when he returns from the

wedding and comes and knocks, they may open to him immediately. 37 Blessed, happy, fortunate, and to be envied are those
servants whom the master finds awake and alert and watching
when he comes. Truly I say to you, he will gird himself and have
them recline at table and will come and serve them! 38 If he
comes in the second watch before midnight or the third watch
after midnight, and finds them so, blessed happy, fortunate, and
to be envied are those servants! 39 But of this be assured: if the
householder had known at what time the burglar was coming, he
would have been awake and alert and watching and would not
have permitted his house to be dug through and broken into. 40
You also must be ready, for the Son of Man is coming at an hour
and a moment when you do not anticipate it.

THE FAITHFUL AND WISE MANAGER

Luke 12:42–48

—————— ❦ ——————

KJV—42 And the Lord said, "Who then is that faithful and wise steward whom his lord shall make ruler over his household, to give them their portion of meat in due season? 43 Blessed is that servant, whom his lord, when he cometh, shall find so doing. 44 Of a truth I say unto you that he will make him ruler over all that he hath. 45 But and if that servant say in his heart, 'My lord delayeth his coming,' and shall begin to beat the menservants and maidens and to eat and drink and to be drunken, 46 the lord of that servant will come in a day when he looketh not for him and at an hour when he is not aware and will cut him in sunder and will appoint him his portion with the unbelievers. 47 And that servant, which knew his lord's will and prepared not himself, neither did according to his will, shall be beaten with many stripes. 48 But he that knew not and did commit things worthy of stripes shall be beaten with few stripes. For unto whomsoever much is given, of him shall be much required, and to whom men have committed much, of him they will ask the more."

Amp—42 And the Lord said, "Who then is that faithful steward, the wise man whom his master will set over those in his household service to supply them their allowance of food at the appointed time? 43 Blessed, happy, and to be envied is that servant whom his master finds so doing when he arrives. 44 Truly I tell you, he will set him in charge over all his possessions. 45 But if that servant says in his heart, 'My master is late in coming,' and begins to strike the menservants and the maids and to eat and drink and get drunk, 46 the master of that servant will come on a day when he does not expect him and at an hour of which he does not know and will punish him and cut him off and assign his lot with the unfaithful. 47 And that servant who knew his master's will but did not get ready or act as he would wish him to act shall be beaten with many lashes. 48 But he who did not know and did things worthy of a beating shall be beaten with few lashes. For everyone to whom much is given, of him shall much be required, and of him to whom men entrust much, they will require and demand all the more."

The Barren Fig Tree

Luke 13:6–9

KJV—6 He spake also this parable: "A certain man had a fig tree planted in his vineyard, and he came and sought fruit thereon and found none. 7 Then said he unto the dresser of his vineyard, 'Behold, these three years I come seeking fruit on this fig tree and find none. Cut it down; why cumbereth it the ground?' 8 And he, answering said unto him, 'Lord, let it alone this year also, till I shall dig about it and dung it. 9 And if it bear fruit, well, and if not, then after that thou shalt cut it down.'"

Amp—6 And he told them this parable: "A certain man had a fig tree planted in his vineyard, and he came looking for fruit on it but did not find any. 7 So he said to the vinedresser, 'See here! For these three years, I have come looking for fruit on this fig tree, and I find none. Cut it down! Why should it continue also to use up the ground to deplete the soil, intercept the sun, and take up room?' 8 But he replied to him, 'Leave it alone, sir, just this one more year, till I dig around it and put manure on the soil. 9 Then perhaps it will bear fruit after this, but if not, you can cut it down and out.'"

THE MUSTARD SEED

Luke 13:18–19

—❧—

KJV—18 Then said he, "Unto what is the kingdom of God like? And whereunto shall I resemble it? 19 It is like a grain of mustard seed, which a man took and cast into his garden, and it grew and waxed a great tree, and the fowls of the air lodged in the branches of it."

Amp—18 This led him to say, "What is the kingdom of God like? And to what shall I compare it? 19 It is like a grain of mustard seed, which a man took and planted in his own garden, and it grew and became a tree, and the wild birds found shelter and roosted and nested in its branches."

THE YEAST

Luke 13:20–21

—⚯—

KJV—20 And again he said, "Whereunto shall I liken the kingdom of God? 21 It is like leaven, which a woman took and hid in three measures of meal, till the whole was leavened."

Amp—20 And again he said, "To what shall I liken the kingdom of God? 21 It is like leaven which a woman took and hid in three measures of wheat flour or meal until it was all leavened fermented."

The Wedding Feast

Luke 14:7–11

—❧—

KJV—7 And he put forth a parable to those which were bidden when he marked how they chose out the chief rooms, saying unto them, 8 "When thou art bidden of any man to a wedding, sit not down in the highest room, lest a more honourable man than thou be bidden of him. 9 And he that bade thee and him come and say to thee, 'Give this man place,' and thou begin with shame to take the lowest room. 10 But when thou art bidden, go and sit down in the lowest room that, when he that bade thee cometh, he may say unto thee, 'Friend, go up higher.' Then shalt thou have worship in the presence of them that sit at meat with thee. 11 For whosoever exalteth himself shall be abased, and he that humbleth himself shall be exalted."

Amp—7 Now he told a parable to those who were invited when he noticed how they were selecting the places of honor, saying to them, 8 "When you are invited by anyone to a marriage feast, do not recline on the chief seat in the place of honor, lest a more distinguished person than you has been invited by him. 9 And he who invited both of you will come to you and say, 'Let this

man have the place you have taken.' Then, with humiliation and
a guilty sense of impropriety, you will begin to take the lowest
place. 10 But when you are invited, go and recline in the lowest place so that, when your host comes in, he may say to you,
'Friend, go up higher!' Then you will be honored in the presence of all who sit at table with you. 11 For everyone who exalts
himself will be humbled ranked below others who are honored
or rewarded, and he who humbles himself, keeps a modest opin-
ion of himself, and behaves accordingly will be exalted, elevated
in rank."

THE GREAT BANQUET

Luke 14:16–24

KJV—16 Then said he unto him, "A certain man made a great supper and bade many 17 and sent his servant at supper time to say to them that were bidden: 'Come, for all things are now ready.' 18 And they all, with one consent, began to make excuse. The first said unto him, 'I have bought a piece of ground, and I must needs go and see it; I pray thee have me excused.' 19 And another said, 'I have bought five yoke of oxen, and I go to prove them; I pray thee have me excused.' 20 And another said, 'I have married a wife, and, therefore, I cannot come.' 21 So that servant came and shewed his lord these things. Then the master of the house, being angry, said to his servant, 'Go out quickly into the streets and lanes of the city, and bring in hither the poor and the maimed and the halt and the blind.' 22 And the servant said, 'Lord, it is done as thou hast commanded, and yet there is room.' 23 And the lord said unto the servant, 'Go out into the highways and hedges, and compel them to come in, that my house may be filled. 24 For I say unto you that none of those men which were bidden shall taste of my supper.'"

Amp—16 But Jesus said to him, "A man was once giving a great supper and invited many, 17 and at the hour for the supper, he sent his servant to say to those who had been invited, 'Come, for all is now ready.' 18 But they all alike began to make excuses and to beg off. The first said to him, 'I have bought a piece of land, and I have to go out and see it; I beg you, have me excused.' 19 And another said, 'I have bought five yoke of oxen, and I am going to examine and put my approval on them; I beg you, have me excused.' 20 And another said, 'I have married a wife, and because of this, I am unable to come.' 21 So the servant came and reported these answers to his master. Then the master of the house said in wrath to his servant, 'Go quickly into the great streets and the small streets of the city, and bring in here the poor and the disabled and the blind and the lame.' 22 And the servant returning, said, 'Sir, what you have commanded me to do has been done, and yet there is room.' 23 Then the master said to the servant, 'Go out into the highways and hedges and urge and constrain them to yield and come in so that my house may be filled. 24 For I tell you, not one of those who were invited shall taste my supper.'"

The Tower Builder

Luke 14:28–30

KJV—28 For which of you, intending to build a tower, sitteth not down first and counteth the cost, whether he have sufficient to finish it? 29 Lest haply, after he hath laid the foundation and is not able to finish it, all that behold it begin to mock him, 30 saying, "This man began to build and was not able to finish."

Amp—28 For which of you, wishing to build a farm building, does not first sit down and calculate the cost to see whether he has sufficient means to finish it? 29 Otherwise, when he has laid the foundation and is unable to complete the building, all who see it will begin to mock and jeer at him, 30 saying, "This man began to build and was not able worth enough to finish."

THE WARRING KING

Luke 14:31–33

———— ✽ ————

KJV—31 Or what king, going to make war against another king, sitteth not down first and consulteth whether he be able, with ten thousand, to meet him that cometh against him with twenty thousand? 32 Or else, while the other is yet a great way off, he sendeth an ambassage and desireth conditions of peace. 33 So likewise, whosoever he be of you that forsaketh not all that he hath, he cannot be my disciple.

Amp—31 Or what king, going out to engage in conflict with another king, will not first sit down and consider and take counsel whether he is able, with ten thousand men, to meet him who comes against him with twenty thousand? 32 And if he cannot do so, when the other king is still a great way off, he sends an envoy and asks the terms of peace. 33 So then, any of you who does not forsake, renounce, surrender claim to, give up, say good-bye to all that he has cannot be my disciple.

THE LOST SHEEP

Luke 15:3–7

KJV—3 And he spake this parable unto them, saying, 4 "What man of you, having an hundred sheep, if he lose one of them, doth not leave the ninety and nine in the wilderness and go after that which is lost until he find it? 5 And when he hath found it, he layeth it on his shoulders, rejoicing. 6 And when he cometh home, he calleth together his friends and neighbours, saying unto them, 'Rejoice with me, for I have found my sheep which was lost.' 7 I say unto you that likewise joy shall be in heaven over one sinner that repenteth, more than over ninety and nine just persons, which need no repentance."

Amp—3 So He told them this parable: 4 "What man of you, if he has a hundred sheep and should lose one of them, does not leave the ninety-nine in the wilderness desert and go after the one that is lost until he finds it? 5 And when he has found it, he lays it on his own shoulders, rejoicing. 6 And when he gets home, he summons together his friends and his neighbors, saying to them, 'Rejoice with me, because I have found my sheep which was lost.' 7 Thus, I tell you, there will be more joy in heaven over one

especially wicked person who repents, changes his mind, abhor-
ring his errors and misdeeds and determines to enter upon a
better course of life than over ninety-nine righteous persons
who have no need of repentance."

The Lost Coin

Luke 15:8–10

———— ✥ ————

KJV—8 Either what woman having ten pieces of silver, if she lose one piece, doth not light a candle and sweep the house and seek diligently till she find it? 9 And when she hath found it, she calleth her friends and her neighbours together, saying, "Rejoice with me, for I have found the piece which I had lost." 10 Likewise, I say unto you, there is joy in the presence of the angels of God over one sinner that repenteth.

Amp—8 Or what woman, having ten silver drachmas, each one equal to a day's wages, if she loses one coin, does not light a lamp and sweep the house and look carefully and diligently until she finds it? 9 And when she has found it, she summons her women friends and neighbors, saying, "Rejoice with me, for I have found the silver coin which I had lost." 10 Even so, I tell you, there is joy among and in the presence of the angels of God over one especially wicked person who repents, changes his mind for the better, heartily amending his ways, with abhorrence of his past sins.

THE PRODIGAL SON

Luke 15:11–32

———— ❧ ————

KJV—11 And he said, "A certain man had two sons. 12 And the younger of them said to his father, 'Father, give me the portion of goods that falleth to me.' And he divided unto them his living. 13 And not many days after the younger son gathered all together and took his journey into a far country and there wasted his substance with riotous living. 14 And when he had spent all, there arose a mighty famine in that land, and he began to be in want. 15 And he went and joined himself to a citizen of that country, and he sent him into his fields to feed swine. 16 And he would fain have filled his belly with the husks that the swine did eat and no man gave unto him. 17 And when he came to himself, he said, 'How many hired servants of my father's have bread enough and to spare, and I perish with hunger! 18 I will arise and go to my father and will say unto him, "Father, I have sinned against heaven and before thee 19 and am no more worthy to be called thy son; make me as one of thy hired servants.' 20 And he arose and came to his father. But when he was yet a great way off, his father saw him and had compassion and ran and fell on his neck and kissed him. 21 And the son said unto him, 'Father, I have sinned against heaven and in thy sight and am no more worthy to be called thy son.' 22 But the father said to his servants, 'Bring forth the best robe, and put it on him; and put a ring on his hand and shoes on his feet. 23 And bring hither the fatted calf, and kill it, and let us eat and be merry. 24 For this, my son, was dead and is alive again; he was lost and is found.' And they began to be merry. 25 Now his elder son was in the field, and as he came and drew nigh to the house, he heard musick and dancing. 26 And he called one of the servants and asked what these things meant. 27 And he said unto him, 'Thy brother is come, and thy father hath killed the fatted calf because he hath received him safe and sound.' 28 And he was angry and would not go in; therefore, came his father out, and intreated him. 29 And he, answering, said to his father, 'Lo, these many years do I serve thee, neither transgressed I at any time thy commandment, and yet thou never gavest me a kid that I might make merry with my friends. 30 But as soon as this, thy son was come, which hath devoured thy living with harlots, thou hast killed for him the fatted calf.' 31 And he said unto him, 'Son, thou art ever with me, and all that I have is thine. 32 It was meet that we should make merry and be glad, for this, thy brother, was dead and is alive again and was lost and is found.'"

Amp—11 And he said, "There was a certain man who had two sons, 12 and the younger of them said to his father, 'Father, give me the part of the property that falls to me.' And he divided the estate between them. 13 And not many days after that, the younger son gathered up all that he had and journeyed into a distant country, and there he wasted his fortune in reckless and loose from restraint living. 14 And when he had spent all he had, a mighty famine came upon that country, and he began to fall behind and be in want. 15 So he went and forced [glued] himself upon one of the citizens of that country, who sent him into his fields to feed hogs. 16 And he would gladly have fed on and filled his belly with the carob pods that the hogs were eating, but they could not satisfy his hunger and nobody gave him anything better. 17 Then when he came to himself, he said, 'How many hired servants of my father have enough food, and even food to spare, but I am perishing, dying here of hunger! 18 I will get up and go to my father, and I will say to him, "Father, I have sinned against heaven and in your sight. 19 I am no longer worthy to be called your son; just make me like one of your hired servants."' 20 So he got up and came to his own father. But while he was still a long way off, his father saw him and was moved with pity and tenderness for him, and he ran and embraced him and kissed him fervently. 21 And the son said to him, 'Father, I have sinned against heaven and in your sight; I am no longer worthy to be called your son. I no longer deserve to be recognized as a son of yours!' 22 But the father said to his bond servants, 'Bring quickly the best robe, the festive robe of honor, and put it on him, and give him a ring for his hand and sandals for his feet. 23 And bring out that wheat fattened calf, and kill it, and let us revel and feast and be happy and make merry, 24 because this, my son, was dead and is alive again; he was lost and is found!' And they began to revel and feast and make merry. 25 But his older son was in the field, and as he returned and came near the house, he heard music and dancing. 26 And having called one of the servant boys to him, he began to ask what this meant. 27 And he said to him, 'Your brother has come, and your father has killed that wheat fattened calf because he has received him back safe and well.' 28 But the elder brother was angry with deep seated wrath and resolved not to go in. Then his father came out and began to plead with him, 29 but he answered his father, 'Look! These many years I have served you, and I have never disobeyed your command. Yet you never gave me so much as a little kid that I might revel and feast and be happy and make merry with my friends, 30 but when this son of yours arrived, who has devoured your estate with immoral women, you have killed for him that wheat fattened calf!' 31 And the father said to him, Son, you are always with me, and all that is mine is yours. 32 But it was fitting to make merry, to revel and feast and rejoice, for this brother of yours was dead and is alive again! He was lost and is found.'"

THE SHREWD MANAGER

Luke 16:1–13

———— ❧ ————

KJV—1 And he said also unto his disciples, "There was a certain rich man, which had a steward, and the same was accused unto him that he had wasted his goods. 2 And he called him and said unto him, 'How is it that I hear this of thee? Give an account of thy stewardship, for thou mayest be no longer steward.' 3 Then the steward said within himself, 'What shall I do? For my lord taketh away from me the stewardship. I cannot dig; to beg I am ashamed. 4 I am resolved what to do, that, when I am put out of the stewardship, they may receive me into their houses.' 5 So he called every one of his lord's debtors unto him and said unto the first, 'How much owest thou unto my lord?' 6 And he said, 'An hundred measures of oil.' And he said unto him, 'Take thy bill, and sit down quickly, and write fifty.' 7 Then said he to another, 'And how much owest thou?' And he said, 'An hundred measures of wheat.' And he said unto him, 'Take thy bill, and write fourscore.' 8 And the lord commended the unjust steward because he had done wisely, for the children of this world are in their generation wiser than the children of light. 9 And I say unto you, make to yourselves friends of the mammon of unrighteousness that, when ye fail, they may receive you into everlasting habitations. 10 He that is faithful in that which is least is faithful also in much, and he that is unjust in the least is unjust also in much. 11 If, therefore, ye have not been faithful in the unrighteous mammon, who will commit to your trust the true riches? 12 And if ye have not been faithful in that which is another man's, who shall give you that which is your own? 13 No servant can serve two masters, for either he will hate the one and love the other, or else he will hold to the one and despise the other. Ye cannot serve God and mammon."

Amp—1 Also Jesus said to the disciples, "There was a certain rich man who had a manager of his estate, and accusations against this man were brought to him that he was squandering his master's possessions. 2 And he called him and said to him, 'What is this that I hear about you? Turn in the account of your management of my affairs, for you can be my manager no longer.' 3 And the manager of the estate said to himself, 'What shall I do, seeing that my master is taking the management away from me? I am not able to dig, and I am ashamed to beg. 4 I have come to know what I will do so that they my master's debtors may accept and welcome me into their houses when I am put out of the management.' 5 So he summoned his master's debtors one by one, and he said to the first, 'How much do you owe my master?' 6 He said, 'A hundred measures, about 900 gallons of oil.' And he said to him, 'Take back your written acknowledgement of obligation, and sit down quickly and write fifty, [about 450 gallons].' 7 After that he said to another, 'And how much do you owe?' He said, 'A hundred measures [about 900 bushels of wheat].' He said to him, 'Take back your written acknowledgement of obligation, and write eighty, [about 700 bushels].' 8 And his master praised the dishonest unjust manager for acting shrewdly and prudently, for the sons of this age are shrewder and more prudent and wiser in relation to their own generation, to their own age and kind, than are the sons of light. 9 And I tell you, make friends for yourselves by means of unrighteous mammon [deceitful riches, money, possessions] so that, when it fails, they those you have favored may receive and welcome you into the everlasting habitations dwellings. 10 He who is faithful in a very little thing is faithful also in much, and he who is dishonest and unjust in a very little thing is dishonest and unjust also in much. 11 Therefore, if you have not been faithful in the case of unrighteous mammon deceitful riches, money, possessions, who will entrust to you the true riches?

12 And if you have not proved faithful in that which belongs to another, whether God or man, who will give you that which is your own, that is the true riches? 13 No servant is able to serve two masters, for either he will hate the one and love the other, or he will stand by and be devoted to the one and despise the other. You cannot serve God and mammon riches or anything in which you trust and on which you rely."

The Rich Man Lazarus

Luke 16:19–31

KJV—19 There was a certain rich man, which was clothed in purple and fine linen and fared sumptuously every day. 20 And there was a certain beggar named Lazarus, which was laid at his gate, full of sores, 21 and desiring to be fed with the crumbs which fell from the rich man's table; moreover, the dogs came and licked his sores. 22 And it came to pass that the beggar died and was carried by the angels into Abraham's bosom; the rich man also died and was buried, 23 and in hell, he lift up his eyes, being in torments, and seeth Abraham afar off and Lazarus in his bosom. 24 And he cried and said, "Father Abraham, have mercy on me, and send Lazarus, that he may dip the tip of his finger in water and cool my tongue, for I am tormented in this flame." 25 But Abraham said, "Son, remember that thou in thy lifetime receivedst thy good things, and likewise Lazarus evil things, but now he is comforted, and thou art tormented. 26 And beside all this, between us and you, there is a great gulf fixed so that they which would pass from hence to you cannot; neither can they pass to us, that would come from thence." 27 Then he said, "I pray thee, therefore, Father, that thou wouldest send him

to my father's house, 28 for I have five brethren that he may tes-
tify unto them, lest they also come into this place of torment." 29
Abraham saith unto him, "They have Moses and the prophets;
let them hear them." 30 And he said, "Nay, Father Abraham, but
if one went unto them from the dead, they will repent." 31 And
he said unto him, "If they hear not Moses and the prophets, neither will they be persuaded, though one rose from the dead."

Amp—19 There was a certain rich man who habitually clothed
himself in purple and fine linen and reveled and feasted and
made merry in splendor every day. 20 And at his gate, there
was carelessly dropped down and left a certain utterly destitute
man named Lazarus, reduced to begging alms and covered with
ulcerated sores. 21 He eagerly desired to be satisfied with what
fell from the rich man's table; moreover, the dogs even came
and licked his sores. 22 And it occurred that the man reduced to
begging died and was carried by the angels to Abraham's bosom.
The rich man also died and was buried. 23 And in Hades, the
realm of the dead, being in torment, he lifted up his eyes and saw
Abraham far away and Lazarus in his bosom. 24 And he cried
out and said, "Father Abraham, have pity and mercy on me, and
send Lazarus to dip the tip of his finger in water and cool my
tongue, for I am in anguish in this flame." 25 But Abraham said,
"Child, remember that you in your lifetime fully received what
is due you in comforts and delights, and Lazarus in like manner
the discomforts and distresses, but now he is comforted here,
and you are in anguish. 26 And besides all this, between us and
you, a great chasm has been fixed in order that those who want
to pass from this place to you may not be able, and no one may
pass from there to us." 27 And the man said, "Then, Father, I
beseech you to send him to my father's house, 28 for I have five

brothers so that he may give solemn testimony and warn them, lest they too come into this place of torment." 29 But Abraham said, "They have Moses and the prophets; let them hear and listen to them." 30 But he answered, "No, Father Abraham, but if someone from the dead goes to them, they will repent, change their minds for the better, and heartily amend their ways, with abhorrence of their past sins." 31 He said to him, "If they do not hear and listen to Moses and the prophets, neither will they be persuaded and convinced and believe even if someone should rise from the dead."

The Master and the Servant

Luke 17:7–10

———— ❧ ————

KJV—7 But which of you, having a servant plowing or feeding cattle, will say unto him by and by, when he is come from the field, "Go and sit down to meat?" 8 And will not rather say unto him, "Make ready wherewith I may sup and gird thyself, and serve me till I have eaten and drunken; and afterward thou shalt eat and drink?" 9 Doth he thank that servant because he did the things that were commanded him? I trow not. 10 So likewise, ye, when ye shall have done all those things which are commanded you, say, "We are unprofitable servants; we have done that which was our duty to do."

Amp—7 Will any man of you who has a servant plowing or tending sheep say to him when he has come in from the field, "Come at once, and take your place at the table?" 8 Will he not instead tell him, "Get my supper ready, and gird yourself and serve me while I eat and drink; then afterward, you yourself shall eat and drink?" 9 Is he grateful and does he praise the servant because he did what he was ordered to do? 10 Even so on your part, when you have done everything that was assigned and commanded you, say, "We are unworthy servants possessing no merit, for we have not gone beyond our obligation; we have merely done what was our duty to do."

The Unjust Judge

Luke 18:1–8

KJV—1 And he spake a parable unto them to this end, that men ought always to pray and not to faint, 2 saying, "There was in a city a judge, which feared not God, neither regarded man. 3 And there was a widow in that city, and she came unto him, saying, 'Avenge me of mine adversary.' 4 And he would not for a while, but afterward, he said within himself, 'Though I fear not God nor regard man, 5 yet because this widow troubleth me, I will avenge her, lest by her continual coming she weary me.' 6 And the Lord said, 'Hear what the unjust judge saith. 7 And shall not God avenge his own elect, which cry day and night unto him, though he bear long with them? 8 I tell you that he will avenge them speedily. Nevertheless when the Son of man cometh, shall he find faith on the earth?'"

Amp—1 Also Jesus told them a parable to the effect that they ought always to pray and not to turn coward, faint, lose heart, and give up. 2 He said, "In a certain city, there was a judge who neither reverenced and feared God nor respected or considered man. 3 And there was a widow in that city who kept coming to him and saying, 'Protect and defend and give me justice against my adversary.' 4 And for a time he would not, but later he said to himself, 'Though I have neither reverence or fear for God nor respect or consideration for man, 5 yet because this widow continues to bother me, I will defend and protect and avenge her, lest she give me intolerable annoyance and wear me out by her continual coming or, at the last, she come and rail on me or assault me or strangle me.' 6 Then the Lord said, 'Listen to what the unjust judge says! 7 And will not our just God defend and protect and avenge his elect, his chosen ones, who cry to him day and night? Will he defer them and delay help on their behalf? 8 I tell you, he will defend and protect and avenge them speedily. However, when the Son of man comes, will he find persistence in faith on the earth?'"

The Pharisee and the Tax Collector

Luke 18:9–14

—⟨⟩—

KJV—9 And he spake this parable unto certain which trusted in themselves that they were righteous and despised others: 10 "Two men went up into the temple to pray; the one a Pharisee and the other a publican. 11 The Pharisee stood and prayed thus with himself, 'God, I thank thee that I am not as other men are: extortioners, unjust, adulterers, or even as this publican. 12 I fast twice in the week; I give tithes of all that I possess.' 13 And the publican, standing afar off, would not lift up so much as his eyes unto heaven but smote upon his breast, saying, 'God be merciful to me a sinner.' 14 I tell you, this man went down to his house, justified rather than the other, for every one that exalteth himself shall be abased, and he that humbleth himself shall be exalted."

Amp—9 He also told this parable to some people who trusted in themselves and were confident that they were righteous that they were upright and in right standing with God and scorned and made nothing of all the rest of men: 10 "Two men went up into the temple enclosure to pray, the one a Pharisee and the other a tax collector. 11 The Pharisee took his stand ostentatiously and began to pray thus before and with himself: 'God, I thank you that I am not like the rest of men: extortioners, robbers, swindlers, unrighteous in heart and life, adulterers, or even like this tax collector here. 12 I fast twice a week; I give tithes of all that I gain.' 13 But the tax collector, merely standing at a distance, would not even lift up his eyes to heaven but kept striking his breast, saying, 'O God, be favorable be gracious, be merciful to me, the especially wicked sinner that I am!' 14 I tell you, this man went down to his home, justified forgiven, and made upright and in right standing with God, rather than the other man, for everyone who exalts himself will be humbled, but he who humbles himself will be exalted."

THE TEN MINAS

Luke 19:12–27

KJV—12 He said, therefore, "A certain nobleman went into a far country to receive for himself a kingdom and to return. 13 And he called his ten servants and delivered them ten pounds, and said unto them, 'Occupy till I come.' 14 But his citizens hated him and sent a message after him, saying, 'We will not have this man to reign over us.' 15 And it came to pass that, when he was returned, having received the kingdom, then he commanded these servants to be called unto him, to whom he had given the money, that he might know how much every man had gained by trading. 16 Then came the first, saying, 'Lord, thy pound hath gained ten pounds.' 17 And he said unto him, 'Well, thou good servant, because thou hast been faithful in a very little, have thou authority over ten cities.' 18 And the second came, saying, 'Lord, thy pound hath gained five pounds.' 19 And he said likewise to him, 'Be thou also over five cities.' 20 And another came, saying, 'Lord, behold, here is thy pound, which I have kept laid up in a napkin, 21 for I feared thee, because thou art an austere man; thou takest up that thou layedst not down and reapest that thou didst not sow.' 22 And he saith unto him, 'Out of thine own mouth will I judge thee, thou wicked servant. Thou knewest that I was an austere man, taking up that I laid not down and reaping that I did not sow. 23 Wherefore then gavest not thou my money into the bank, that at my coming I might have required mine own with usury?' 24 And he said unto them that stood by, 'Take from him the pound, and give it to him that hath ten pounds.' 25 And they said unto him, 'Lord, he hath ten pounds.' 26 For I say unto you, 'That unto every one which hath shall be given, and from him that hath not, even that he hath shall be taken away from him. 27 But those mine enemies, which would not that I should reign over them, bring hither, and slay them before me.'"

Amp—12 He therefore said, "A certain nobleman went into a distant country to obtain for himself a kingdom and then to return. 13 Calling ten of his own bond servants, he gave them ten minas, each equal to about one hundred days' wages or nearly twenty dollars and said to them, 'Buy and sell with these while I go and then return.' 14 But his citizens detested him and sent an embassy after him to say, 'We do not want this man to become ruler over us.' 15 When he returned after having received the kingdom, he ordered these bond servants to whom he had given the money to be called to him, that he might know how much each one had made by buying and selling. 16 The first one came before him, and he said, 'Lord, your mina has made ten additional minas.' 17 And he said to him, 'Well done, excellent bond servant! Because you have been faithful and trustworthy in a very little thing, you shall have authority over ten cities.' 18 The second one also came and said, 'Lord, your mina has made five more minas.' 19 And he said also to him, 'And you will take charge over five cities.' 20 Then another came and said, 'Lord, here is your mina, which

I have kept laid up in a handkerchief. 21 For I was constantly afraid of you, because you are a stern hard, severe man; you pick up what you did not lay down, and you reap what you did not sow.' 22 He said to the servant, 'I will judge and condemn you out of your own mouth, you wicked slave! You knew [did you] that I was a stern, hard, severe man, picking up what I did not lay down and reaping what I did not sow? 23 Then why did you not put my money in a bank so that, on my return, I might have collected it with interest?' 24 And he said to the bystanders, 'Take the mina away from him, and give it to him who has the ten minas.' 25 And they said to him, 'Lord, he has ten minas already!'" 26 And said Jesus, "I tell you that to everyone who gets and has will more be given, but from the man who does not get and does not have, even what he has will be taken away. 27 The indignant king ended by saying 'But as for these enemies of mine who did not want me to reign over them, bring them here, and slaughter them in my presence.'"

The Tenants

Luke 20:9–16

———— ❈ ————

KJV—9 Then began he to speak to the people this parable: A certain man planted a vineyard and let it forth to husbandmen and went into a far country for a long time. 10 And at the season, he sent a servant to the husbandmen, that they should give him of the fruit of the vineyard, but the husbandmen beat him and sent him away empty. 11 And again he sent another servant, and they beat him also and entreated him shamefully and sent him away empty. 12 And again he sent a third, and they wounded him also and cast him out. 13 Then said the lord of the vineyard, "What shall I do? I will send my beloved son; it may be they will reverence him when they see him." 14 But when the husbandmen saw him, they reasoned among themselves, saying, "This is the heir; come, let us kill him that the inheritance may be ours." 15 So they cast him out of the vineyard and killed him. What, therefore, shall the lord of the vineyard do unto them? 16 He shall come and destroy these husbandmen and shall give the vineyard to others. And when they heard it, they said, "God forbid."

Amp—9 Then he began to relate to the people this parable, this story, to figuratively portray what he had to say: A man planted a vineyard and leased it to some vinedressers and went into another country for a long stay. 10 When the right season came, he sent a bond servant to the tenants, that they might give him his part of the fruit of the vineyard, but the tenants beat, thrashed him and sent him away empty handed. 11 And he sent still another servant; him they also beat, thrashed, and dishonored and insulted him disgracefully and sent him away empty-handed. 12 And he sent yet a third; this one they wounded and threw out of the vineyard. 13 Then the owner of the vineyard said, "What shall I do? I will send my beloved son; it is probable that they will respect him." 14 But when the tenants saw him, they argued among themselves, saying, "This is the heir; let us kill him so that the inheritance may be ours." 15 So they drove him out of the vineyard and killed him. What then will the owner of the vineyard do to them? 16 He will come and utterly put an end to those tenants and will give the vineyard to others. When they, the chief priests and the scribes and the elders heard this, they said, "May it never be."

THE FIG TREE

Luke 21:29–33

———— ❧ ————

KJV—29 And he spake to them a parable: Behold the fig tree and all the trees; 30 when they now shoot forth, ye see and know of your own selves that summer is now nigh at hand. 31 So likewise ye, when ye see these things come to pass, know ye that the kingdom of God is nigh at hand. 32 Verily I say unto you, this generation shall not pass away till all be fulfilled. 33 Heaven and earth shall pass away, but my words shall not pass away.

Amp—29 And he told them a parable: Look at the fig tree and all the trees; 30 when they put forth their buds and come out in leaf, you see for yourselves and perceive and know that summer is already near. 31 Even so, when you see these things taking place, understand and know that the kingdom of God is at hand. 32 Truly I tell you, this generation, those living at that definite period of time will not perish and pass away until all has taken place. 33 The sky and the earth, the universe, the world will pass away, but my words will not pass away.

And he said, "Unto you, it is given to know the mysteries of the kingdom of God but to others in parables, that seeing they might not see and hearing they might not understand." Luke 8:10

OTHER BOOKS BY THE AUTHOR

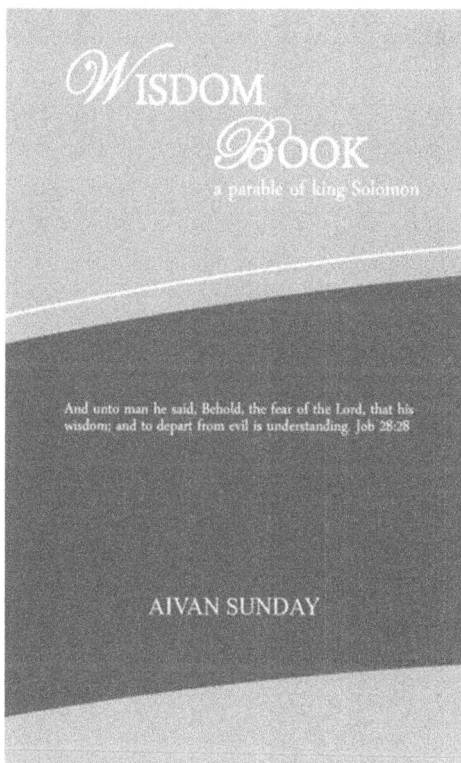

Prayer for salvation and baptism in the Holy Spirit

Righteous Father, I come to you in the name of Jesus. Your word
says whosoever shall call on the name of the Lord shall be saved

(Acts 2:21). I am calling on you. I pray and ask Jesus to come into my heart and be lord over my life according to Romans 10:9–10. If thou shalt confess with thy mouth the Lord Jesus and shalt believe in thine heart that God hath raised him from the dead, thou shalt be saved. Dear Jesus, I believe that you died for me and rose again on the third day. I confess I am a sinner. I need your love and forgiveness; come into my heart, and forgive my sins. By giving me peace, joy, and supernatural love for others, I receive your eternal life and confirm your love. Amen

I am also asking you, Lord, to fill me with the Holy Spirit. Holy Spirit, rise up within me as I praise God.

ABOUT THE AUTHOR

Aivan Osarobo Sunday is founder and senior pastor of King Jesus Ministries UK. An anointed songwriter and the author of several books, including Wisdom Book: A Parable of King Solomon, he is passionate about following his calling to teach the good news of God's kingdom to all the nations and prepare Christians for the return of Jesus Christ.

To learn more about the author and ministry:

9 Haddington Drive Manchester
M9 6LR England, United Kingdom
E-mail: info@kingjesusministries.co.uk
Website: www.kingjesusministries.co.uk
Telephone: +44 7950913053

www.ingramcontent.com/pod-product-compliance
Lightning Source LLC
Chambersburg PA
CBHW070638030426
42337CB00020B/4065